NAPE

NAPE

Jan Seale

ISBN: 978-0-9835968-6-8
Library of Congress Control Number: 2011934338

Cover art: Erren Seale
Manufactured in the United States

Ink Brush Press
Temple and Dallas, Texas

Acknowledgements

The author gratefully acknowledges the first publication of
some of the poems in this volume by the following journals and
anthologies:

*Concho River Review, Crab Creek Review, Cries of the Spirit,
Isosceles, Latitude 30° 18', Mixed Voices: Contemporary Poems
About Music, Native Soil: poems from South Texas poets,
Plumbline, Raintown Review, RiverSedge, Southwestern
American Literature, Texas in Poetry II, Texas Poets in Concert:
A Quartet, The Cape Rock, The Student, The Texas Observer,
The Wonder Is: New and Selected Poems 1974-2004,
Valleysong, Visions: International*

Poetry from Ink Brush Press

Alan Birkelbach and Karla Morton, *No End of Vision: Texas as Seen by Two Laureates*
Jerry Bradley, *The Importance of Elsewhere*
Millard Dunn, *Places We Could Never Find Alone*
Chris Ellery, *The Big Mosque of Mercy*
Charles Inge, *Brazos View*
Steven Schroeder, *a dim sum of the day before*
Steven Schroeder and Sou Vai Keng, *a guest giving way like ice melting*
Jan Seale, *The Wonder Is*
W.K. Stratton. *Dreaming Sam Peckinpah*
Chuck Taylor, *At the Heart*
Jesse Waters, *Human Resources*

For information on these and other Ink Brush Press books go to www.inkbrushpress.com

to those everywhere

who struggle

to name and to bear the Light

CONTENTS

I. Gatherings

II. Marvels

III. Harmonies

IV. Volitions

V. Futures

I. Gatherings

Everybody likes to go their own way—
to choose their own time and manner of devotion.

—Jane Austen
(1775-1817)
Mansfield Park

How the Grandmother of the World will Entertain Herself

Each time they skitter, soar, float, circle,
birds leave a line on the air. Meanwhile,
She is making of these a tight string ball.

At the last, the Grandmother of the World
will stoop, open the bottom drawer,
shake off thumbtacks and bread wrapper ties,
retrieve the ball. She'll rise slowly—
the Ages make for arthritis—and begin to unwind,
rearranging the bird paths to Her liking:

First, those that squawk, scold, screech, quack.
Next will be hoots, chirks, caws
followed by whistles, trills,
and finally, mere coos.

Then the Grandmother of the World will
stand satisfied, the string in a nest at Her feet,
the only sound the whisper of dreaming feathers.

Matins, still dark

a town first awakens the people with bells
a town calls loud for God with bells
a town speaks glossolalia in bells
a town attends a party of bells
a town makes love to bells
a town delirious in bells
a town chatting in bells
a town cross with bells
a town sad with bells

a town in a final competition of bells
loose, crying, murdering with bells
a town, town, town
a few bells
two bells
bell

Baptism 1976

That Sunday I ovulated during morning grace,
ping and plosion from one ovary, twinge of a world,
only one less of my thousands; nevertheless,
it was a sign, some oracle of things to come.
Later I sat in church. Infant baptism.
Female infant baptism.
A sister in Christ weighing 15 pounds.
Tamara Lynn Hassock, daughter
of Mr. and Mrs. P.N. Hassock,
Guest Minister Today.
She gave the object lesson, the fabliau, the hortatory
looking out over the black velvet of the priest's shawl
in her antique christening dress.
Her message was this:
      Hiccup!
     "God the Father"
       Hiccup!
     "God the King"
         Hiccup!
       "God the Lord"
       Hiccup Hiccup Hiccup!

I thank Tamara for expressing most subtly
my state of digestion under the Hebrew patriarchs.

Jan Seale

How the Wax Churches of Los Aztecas Bloom

When the air is dry and the day not too hot too cold
when the table is brought and placed four-square
in the center of the *ejido* and on it a bowl of water

when the world has lasted another year *Gracias a Dios*
because *La Virgen de la Inmaculada Concepción*
has interceded for the village of Los Aztecas and
Our Lady's festival is set for the eighth of December

when reeds are gathered from beside the Rio Guayalejo
and left to ripen then stripped and made into bases
with rising walls saving space for windows and doors
all leading heavenward by towers to roofs and crosses

when three dies of mesquite are brought from the trunk
where they live out generations wrapped in rags
except for these their own feast days and
are soaked in water and watched over for a small while

when the dyed bee's wax in the copper pan over the fire
rouses from last year's lump but does not smoke
and by the goat-footed grace of the artisan
arrives safe at the table over the hard ground

when the children are assembled at a distance
a few boys with sticks against the curious pigs
the women in doorways their arms full of babies
their heads draped in dish towels against the sun

when Pánfilo Vázquez Fondón takes up a die
with his tongs and dips it in the sun of bee's wax
with help from the ghost of his mother

4

who has help from the ghost of her father
who practiced this art in San Luis Potosí

and when the face of the die is coated with wax
and quickly held high like a crucifix by Pánfilo
who then brings it down to his mouth and blows thrice
Padre   Hijo   Espíritu Santo
peels the wax like the membrane of a newborn
baptizes his child in the bowl and then dries it

when he has enough stacks of patterns and colors
and when his friend Tranquilina from Palmillas
delivers him her wax flowers and bells the art of which
she had to leave her unsympathetic husband in order to save

when Pánfilo assembles all this in the storage *jacal*
and with a small fire going outside begins to attach
the filigreed segments one by one to the reed frame
handling each piece of wax as a butterfly or hot coal
as a bird's egg as snow as a silk ribbon as a kiss
his breath hardly taken and never the eyes off the work

reaching out sideways to the boy who will be there
to place the new ember in his hand until the corner
of one piece hangs to the cane then fuses with another
its neighbor until there is a transept of bright pink

like the roses clutched to the breast of *La Virgen*
and twin belfries webbed green as the grass at her feet
the windows and doors a white lace of her reputation
the roof fashioned of Our Lady of Heaven's blue mantle

when the churches all forty are finished so that word is sent
for Señoras Zarate and Canales and Apolado to fetch them
each taking her own church away on her head

5

Jan Seale

Pánfilo standing in the doorway smiling and sighing
"*Adiós mis jardincitos*" watching his little gardens march
straightaway each made with a difference detectable
only to himself because he has pledged it to God

when at last the eighth of December comes with veneration
of *La Virgen de la Inmaculada Concepción* who makes all
that is good to happen the rest of the year in Los Aztecas

and Pánfilo's wax churches are seen on the heads
of the faithful in the *parada* amidst the standards floating
with ribbons and children bearing scarves and priests
with headpieces and dancers Aztecas and the statue of *La Virgen*

when the time is over for the divine grillwork
for the arches scallops webs eyelets curves flowers
for the angles windows doors roofs and bells

and Pánfilo sits late in the night rubbing his eyes seeing
inside them his churches high on the heads of the faithful
in the brilliant midday how beautiful how beautiful
the *jardincito*s of Los Aztecas this year how beautiful

when Pánfilo has allowed his heart to soar to heaven
in the arms of *La Virgen de la Inmaculada Concepción*

then and only then does he give the sign
for the small greedy hands to tear the lace
from the frameworks throwing all into piles of color
breaking the frameworks of reeds to feed the fires
all the while Pánfilo hearing the laughter of destruction

it is then he melts down the mounds of lace to store
the lumps in cool jars sleeping away from the light

6

thinking how next year he will lay the fire
how he will stir the wax clods into swirling sky

how his hands will become the hands of the sower
scattering the seeds of sacrifice on Our Lady's altar
new and more beautiful churches offered up to her
these little gardens of his heart pleasing her

each piece of lace hearing the echo of its mother
out of the cold lump heating over the fire
each reed hearing from the crackling bonfire
of death its father of the year before

the freshest and most beautiful of bouquets springing
with gratitude and entreaty new ever new.

Jan Seale

Chapel

The soldier's ears sprout pink below the hair
cut one-half inch to army regulation;
they scoop up headgearsful of words the prayer
is programming for later meditation
in the helicopter squatting among the enemy.
Responsive reading number twenty-nine
calls his attention to a speck of oily
stuff beneath his thumbnail which demands the time
spanning the offertory. When next, "Praise God
From Whom All Blessings" sends him to attention
on football legs, back like a ramrod,
does he not look like Jesus of stained-glass ascension?
The sermon is quite long: "How to Be Brave."
Between his ears he contemplates his grave.

Come Celebrate Another Early Snake

Now the serpent was more subtle than any beast
of the field which the Lord God had made.
Genesis 3:1

Come celebrate another early snake—
a garden dweller who did not proffer sin.
Say that being also tended earth's daybreak.

Tell of a woman who did not care to make
a meal of apples and share them with her kin.
Come celebrate another early snake.

Rumor a man who did not know soul-ache
for an odyssey beyond the garden's din.
Say that being also tended earth's daybreak.

Speak a serpent whose head man could not break,
nor mouth would bruise a man's Achilles-skin.
Come celebrate another early snake.

A woman who did not have a thirst to slake
in any juice of tree that might have been—
say that being also tended earth's daybreak.

Know a snake that moved for love's own sake.
Say for Eden's viper was a twin.
Come celebrate another early snake.
Say that being also tended earth's daybreak.

Jan Seale

Feast Day at Jémez

I.
We are the lucky ones, *bolillos* invited to Joyce's pueblo.
It is August 2, the Feast of Our Lady of the Angels
with the Old Pecos Bull Dance, the day donated in 1838
by eighteen poor Pecos come to winter with the Jémez.
Certain outsiders may visit. We are designated friends.
Coming out between dwellings, we are unprepared
for the space, a plaza of sand big as a soccer field.
At the far end Our Lady of the Angels sits in blessing
of a yucca shelter. Transported from the church,
she is comfortable among crosses, flowers.
This is the last time we will see her.

II.
The turquoise order flows in. These are the *tsúnta tabösh.*
They concern themselves with the sprouting of plants.
They are the winter group.
Somewhere down near Our Lady of the Angels,
the *cacique* gives the signal and the drumming begins.
A choir of men, the old in polyester and squash blossoms,
the young in jeans and boots, moves out to the chant
of the Walatowa. The square is washed in color, motion,
like a camouflaged beast flushed from hiding.
Slow feet beginning, sway of bodies, branches waving.
Girls and women smothered in sashes, *sacques, rebozos,*
vests, leggings, crowned in turquoise headpieces;
boys and men in breech cloths, shells like bullet belts
crossing their chests, coyote skins tied to their waists,
fir branches bouncing like show ponies' tails.
Thousands of bells say their prayers in unison.
The dancers do not smile, do not recognize anyone.
This dance is not for tourists. No pictures.
Heat shimmers. The desert praises this lake of color.
We stand bleached to the bone with envy.

III.
Now the squash dancers take their place.
An old man in the chant group growls,
"Back! Back! Can't you see we need room?"
We can't see—don't know the divine plan
but stumble backward over each other,
humbled and guilt-stricken.
Buddy is in the squash chanters.
He greets us, goes solemnly to his work.
Some of the old men move their mouths
hardly at all, perhaps out of boredom,
perhaps to conceal their words from us.
Some of the younger watch the mouths of the old.
It is important to get it right, keep it right.

The drumming, the shuffling begin.
The chinking of bells. The nasal singing.
On and on. On and on. Seductive murmur.
The sun doesn't move all afternoon.
My friends leave for shade.
I look down, the tops of my feet are scorched.
I have not shifted for three hours.
Maybe I am planted.
Maybe this is how they insure the crops.

That night back in my bed in Albuquerque,
I wish the sunburn were pigment.
I wonder how to belong,
how to read the god that drums my heart.

Sand paints me to sleep.

Jan Seale

Christmastide/ the Texican Border

Mild, sheep weather,
star-harboring skies,
a travelers' moon;

stones to pile up,
sit upon, make a fence,
roll away from a tomb;

cicadas singing glorias,
flowering olives for prayer,
fig trees cursed and blessed;

Palma Christi for donkey feet,
for sparrow homes,
for Solomon's sweets;

the passion flower of cacti,
sand to write a message in,
posadas to journey in hope;

and a river, wide and deep,
where, crossing to either side,
we are baptized anew.

II. Marvels

Everything sacred must surround itself in mystery.

—Stéphane Mallarmé
(1842-1898)

Believing Is Seeing

And these signs shall follow them that believe.
                    Mark 16:17

Eyes that have tracked rabbits, birds, deer
all afternoon across the simple oak
now tear and smart, ready as they are
to discover in the cold Hill Country night
Orion among the hot uncompromising stars.

The astronomer emerges from his lens.
"We have a treat tonight," my son says
and waits until a plane has closed its path.
"First you find Orion by his belt."
His finger points me to the spangled girth.

And then we telescope the Great Hunter:
the yellow-red on his right shoulder named
Betelgeuse, a pulsing variable giant,
and Bellatrix on his left; straight down
find Rigel, making his knee a blue-white glint.

We shiver and our breaths form nebulae
of no order. "The next stars"—my son smiles—
"we'll see together. I have to show you how."
I will to see beyond the late-night books,
the fog of years, the dimming earthly weather.

"Beside the sword you'll see a cloudy mass."
I strain through waves and jerks from here to there,
search Orion's skirt for starry soil.
The cloud mass finally settles to its place.
"You mean the thing that looks like printers' dots?"

Jan Seale

"Orion's Nebula," the astronomer says,
then stands against me firm to make a brace.
"Keep looking, Mom. For now, just blink and stare.
I promise you will see them if you try,
and hope—yes, hope for three bright stars."

Minutes go by. The click of the telescope timer
corrects what we cannot—our restless ride
on this galloping star-drenched porch.
And then the gift: three clear and perfect points,
three diamond apples where none were before.

Afraid to blink, I whisper, "Yes, I see them.
Yes." The astronomer's hand tightens on my arm.
"The Trapezium Cluster, at fifteen-hundred light-years."
He laughs. "I give them to you because you see them."
"I take them," I say, and feel him near.

The Fire-eater of Reynosa

As if the eight lanes of NAFTA Peterbilts
and tarp-covered melon trucks
and *camionetas* lined with dusty workers
and sedans of *señoras* headed for bridal showers
and bone-drenched donkeys pulling toothless men
and gaunt boys hopping lanes with bottles of Coca
wasn't enough death waiting to happen,
in the median, with his girlfriend as assistant,
the fire-eater at the last intersection
on the road to the Monterrey cutoff
makes ready.

His eyes are fiery, like the red he wills
on the signal overhead. (He's picked this place
because the red is longest here.) When the sound is
squealing brakes, downshifts, drifting stops,
he drinks naphtha from the pop bottle she holds,
his cheeks bulging in his hairless face,
grabs the sopped torch from her
and prances forward. Clown-ragged, cockeyed,
scarred, he crosses himself, brandishes his torch,
crosses himself twice more.

This is too much! *Loco!*
The motorists honk, rev engines, inch forward.
Murder comes easily into their hearts.
Would serve him right—to barbeque!
If he's not dead when the light goes green,
they'll finish off the job. He's torture.

Posed deadly still, he suddenly spews a fountain,
lights the spray with a flourish of torch.

Jan Seale

Then, then all time stops—no one knows how long—
because from his mouth there's fire,
flame, beautiful shafts of curling orange.
He's dragonesque, waggles his head
to demonstrate complete control.
The intersection has no place to go,
to look away. The fire-eater is
everybody's sight, time, existence.

In the second before the light turns faulty yellow
in its rush toward green, the fire-eater,
sated with his meal of fire, bows,
and bows again, then leaps away.
Half-sick with bitter taste, the fiery column
printed on his retinas, a little drunk,
he and his assistant frolic in shouts, waves,
a rain of coins, an applause of honking.

And those who cursed him seconds ago
take off for Monterrey, unknown to themselves
redeemed, shot out of this strangest of cannons,
refreshed by the spectacle of cheated death,
unable to say anything except
"Holy Jesus! What a fool! What a miracle!"

Grand Mal

First the siren voice untraceable
sending us swivel-necked in alarm,
then outstretched arms toward a place
we cannot go. It will not happen.
This cannot happen to happen
in this place. Haply it does.

THIS CLASSROOM RESERVED
for my questions, your answers.
We come in, sit down,
look at the pale walls,
finger pencils and watches,
discourse on the comma.

Now galvanic overload unlocks us
from our chairs, sends us
to lay her on the floor,
to stand as acolytes
to her hushed suffering—
twitch of feet and nibbling lips,
unpaired eyes and moiling fists—
thanks, she is not here.

Then, after light years
in our blushing hearts
and seeing she lies quiet
on the dirty floor in a sleep
we have to envy, so deep
even her hair asleep,
we go forth Lazaruses
into the hall, out of her storm,
saying only with our eyes that
we have seen a miracle
and are risen.

Scriptural X-Rays, 1905

Each time I take down this Book of
Emblems, Allegories, and Similitudes
the century leaves crumbs in my lap.
Its title page announces it Reveals
the Secrets of the Human Heart
Penetrates the Soul
and Lays Bare the Character
Of Every Man, Woman, and Child.
Only my grandfather's florid signature
of ownership protects me.

Here I will find emblematic engravings
showing the Pain and Misery
Resulting from Vice
and the Peace and Happiness
Arising Out of Virtue. I hope so.

I see Grandfather marching home
to the old Arkansas farmhouse,
smiling at his estate-sale bargain,
these 537 pages tucked securely
under one arm, and looking not unlike
the man in smug top hat
of one engraving who travels bravely
through a cut-away trough
of Clouds and Darkness, Sin and Error.

Soon he'll show my grandmother
(who's frying chicken for the usual nine),
that animals are here depicted bad:
goats of Licentiousness,
pigs of Intemperance,

dogs of Anger and Ill Will,
all slain at the feet of Sanctified Christian,
hands folded, eyes lifted up to heaven.

In The Path of Life and Way of Death,
an elevated road, like the Great Wall of China,
runs through a canyon and steeply up a mountain,
whereat sits a castle, a few brave souls
struggling toward it while a crowd
throngs the foreground, notably distressed
that their brethren and sistern pitch
headlong into a nearby convenient abyss.

If we do not understand the allegory,
we have only to read the labels written on each:
In one precursor of "no pain no gain,"
Large letters say, "No Cross No Crown,"
the crown perched on a mountain peak,
the cross plainly obstructing bewildered earthlings.
(My grandfather says Look a'here,
Look how the artist made the foreground . . .
background . . . made the people *real* between.)

Young women mortals wear Josephine gowns,
have small breasts, prowl demurely, whereas
older matrons, bustle-proud and bonnet-topped,
lean on their courteous Edwardian men.
Poorhouse women look more comfortable,
sleeveless and barefoot, their hair in a bun.

Women angels wear Greek togas,
crowd together with intrusive wings,
sing on high, hold up lanterns
or sit on rocks and point heavenward.
There are exceptions:

Jan Seale

Slander has a snake in her mouth,
one foot barely missing hellish flames.

The men engage in combat row on row;
they're crowned or epauletted.
Charioteers, captains of Viking ships,
they're battling their evil quadruplets:
Self-Will, Folly, Greed, Presumption.
Poor men are also cooler, thin shirts a-flap,
bending in fields with short-handled hoes.

In the midst of all these Scriptural allegories,
here's a specially tinted painting named
"Uncle Sam and the Liquor Dealer."
The two smile and agree about a stone building
with Club Rooms for drinking Fine Whiskey,
while men pour out the back door
in a line for the Poor House.

My grandfather is excited, wants to read
this book 'til bedtime. But supper's ready.
He rises from his cane-bottomed chair,
walks the volume to his study,
lays it on his roll-top desk.
Tomorrow he will write in it:
"Worth every penny I paid for this."
In the corner is the price: 75 good cents.
He's sure of it.
Then, emboldened by his faith,
he writes his standard admonishment:
"Exodus 20:15 Thou Shalt Not Steal."

A Pioneer Preacher Speaks of Cedar
for Lou and Charles

Time was, Preaching and wood agreed
with a man: all week chopping cedar
on the hill; come Sunday, Joshua 9:21—
"hewers of wood and drawers of water."

You had your standards or you didn't.
There'd be no pawning off of posts
with little heartwood, odor, color—
only for writing, this "pencil" cedar.

No sir, God did not easily forgive
a cedar cheater, but blessed He did
the one who rendered posts so strong
they'd last a hundred years or more.

This, from the trees called "Mexican Red,"
and posts you cut from them had worth
just like a statue found in rock.
God sent them straight for bartering.

A load of posts could gain you much:
a hog dressed out, brought to your door;
for the wife: dry goods, sugar, flour;
for the children: music lessons or shoes.

When I die, let my headstone
be a stump of proper cedar,

Jan Seale

and if ever there's a time fence posts
all come out from town, chop anyway.

Make shreds of limbs and berries,
the prickled green, and every chip—
for many's the Christmas after me
will need the touch of nature sure.

And though the moth doth corrupt,
(I have preached it many a time),
still, let the cedar guard your treasures
here on earth—it is no sin.

You need a rest from preaching?
Take your axe to Halsell Hill.
From Word to wood is little distance.
Savor the swing, the split. Be saved.

Charting the Nature Trail

We are walking the path, thinking how to script this world
of thorns and old wood smoking with green-leafed humidity
into something charming and public.

But the place is heavy, mute with August morning.
It is sticking to us—even the names. Too much hackberry,
iron tree, prickly pear in this thornscrub forest.

The lotebush patch is whispering "Brer Rabbit."
Mosquitoes and mesquites conspire. Nothing
is helping us educate the public or philanthropists.

Of real concern is a gangling vegetable mountain,
a cactus acting out at a scenic turn. Gray, meandering,
it's a bizarre TinkerToy straining our limits of "green."

One morning on the trail, early to beat the sun and gnats,
through lonesome bird calls and the tittering leaves
of sick August, we approach . . . white.

Have vandals littered the sanctuary in the night?
A school boy flung his notebook?
Pranksters wrapped the environment with toilet paper?

Closer, we see the truth: The Night-blooming Cereus—
embarrassing acting-out cactus—caught in the act,
partying in a hundred blooms the size of dinner plates.

We've surprised a convention of vain princesses,
a passel of folkloric dancers, their white petticoats twirling,
awaiting the bridegrooms of groveling bees.

From silence the laughter leaks, bubbles over.
In our good fortune, we lay down binoculars, clipboards,
wade into the forest grabbing us, tearing our clothes

to reach the vanilla fragrance, see at close range
the burlesque of stamina, pistils, corollas.
The question rises in our throats:

"If giant white flowers bloom in the thornscrub forest,
and there's no one to see them, are they there?"
And the Great Nanny-Boo-Boo replies, "Be Cereus!"

To a Woman who Pleased King Solomon

You there in the Word,
get out!

You with goblet-belly,
heap of wheat among lilies
and twin-running breasts.

You,
harlot-necked in ivory,
wet-eyed,
night-haired,
smelling of fruit.

Run away!
Get you down the halls
of Jerusalem!

For you were beautiful
and dared dance
in our Holy Scriptures.

Jan Seale

In the Church at Mier

Shadow of Christ on the stone wall,
odor of chrysanthemums,
timid stations of the cross,
pillars thick, stark.

The man speaks:
Do you see *La Virgen*?
What I am about to tell you—
I know better—
but you must believe.
I am an educated man,
without superstitions.
Once, when I was a lonely child,
she cried for me,
a large tear from her marble eye
down the length of her clay face.
Don't ask my explaining!
Her tears were real!

Never, since, has she cried for me.
Never. But I always come to check.
With hope I seek a listener,
tell this story.

Icon
for Don

He waits in the alcove, a station of the cross,
his own—built to hold a wheelchair.

From time to time we step out,
retrieve his bulletin at his feet.

We find the hymn, the Bible passage,
prop these in his lost hands.

This morning he can't say one word
to his wife or any who greet him.

But he can sing the hymn, "For all
the saints who in their order stood."

The high mass of Parkinson's
frames the arched side aisle.

When they bring the Elements to him,
dipping the bread in the wine,

touching his lips with Christ's body,
a storm breaks in him, a whirlwind

on the brain's horizon, clouds of tears
and rumbling out of nowhere.

Time was, this weather startled us,
embarrassed us that it embarrassed him.

Now we are envious, seeing that
the Holy Spirit comes upon him,

that he has moved on beyond us
halfway to heaven through his tears,

singing, prayers—past appearances,
the dignity of the body, the world

of a man's work—Sunday after Sunday
a white shirt, a tie, a pressed suit,

miracle to everyone but himself.
How the Spirit shines out!

How rare and beautiful!
A man brings himself forth

out of darkness each day,
bestowing the gift of awe

on us circling about him.
We would form a line

in the darkened side aisle,
stand with folded hands,

kneel before his chair,
receive a blessing.

Tired hands, mute tongue,
dark eyes speak saint.

III. Harmonies

The music of the Gospel leads us home.

—Frederick William Farber
(1814-1863)

"On Jordan's Stormy Banks . . . "

. . . you do not stand, but in a creek in Arkansas.
The picture man, On Higher Ground,
weds science and faith. We hold you here,
a Sunday 1925, by celluloid and miracle,
a child robed in white, facing baptism
with six more, all saved from hell in spring revival.

Behind you, just out the clapboard church's door,
the congregation stands in solemn witness:
menfolk with collars open, sleeves rolled up,
women in cool batiste, umbrellas shading.
Small boys roll down the cemetery's hill.
Your mother holds the latest baby.

Last week you walked the aisle, faint and weary,
vile and corrupted, sin-sick and sore.
Now you are Washed in the Blood of the Lamb,
in A Fountain Filled With Blood, losing your guilty stain,
your garments about to be spotless, white as snow,
Bound, as you are, for the Promised Land

at eleven years of age, as is your cousin Cecil
now just ahead in line. You two have made a pact:
Looking underwater, you will report your findings.
Agreement insures salvation; if not, you'll fight.
Your teacher in the Sunday School suggested
angels, a cross, or, at the very least, a glowing light.

God knows, baptism does not save. We do
no Pope-ish ritual, no hocus-pocus, no sirree.
Oh yes, the name is Baptist but immersion
is a simple picture of how worldliness is killed.

And Methodist sprinkling is a heresy.
In all this you have been drilled.

Yet when your pa, holding his own revival
one county over, reads from you "Pa, I'm saved.
Should I be baptized, or wait for you?"
he answers: "Son, What does tomorrow bring?
You might go out into eternity tonight.
By all means, be baptized this Sunday eve."

And when you are in position, fingers locked secure
against a sudden panic, and the preacher intones,
"You are buried with Christ," and dunks backward
then lifts you, spewing and a-tremble,
and shouts, "You arise to walk in newness of life!"
you know baptism's more than just a symbol.

Later, after evening service and goodbyes,
homeward on the sandy peach-strewn road,
quarter-mile behind the buggy, you ask your cousin,
"So what did you see?" and, thank God,
Cecil's answer chimes with yours and sends
the two of you to cartwheels of joy.

For though This World Is Not Your Home,
and A Charge To Keep You Have, to Yield
Not to Temptation, and Where He Leads
you must follow if you want Victory in Jesus, still
this afternoon, Down in the Sacred Wave,
you boys agree the Holy Spirit was a turtle.

"Pilgrim! Pilgrim! Why Do You Tarry?"

Bedclothes will do anything
to trap lovers—
tie them up, hand and foot,
insinuate themselves
into the life of the flesh,
beg to get in the game,
threaten to be winding sheets.

Plates with faces of unkempt children,
cups with seductive lips parted,
forks and knives poking and slicing
at the conversation
hope to win some argument,
tell an anecdote,
get in a word edgewise.

And in the garden a rose bush
pouts for a drink,
an elephant ear strives to listen,
and a tomato plant curls its fists
in fatal threat to the spider mite.

These sly bids for attention
you misinterpret.

For every moan of porch swing,
pillow imprinted with lover's head,
cup of coffee steaming gentle as purgatory,
you hear work calling.
It's order! order! you think
you are called to.

Welts from hot soapy water
rise on your arms like stigmata.
Dirt creeps to your nails
like mice to a pantry.
Dead stems and leaves drape you.

You try to be lost
in conversation
thought
or sex.

You think you can ignore
this itch, this finagling
of things that love you,
this kind plotting
of your possessions
to keep you out of
the Devil's workshop.

"Work, for the Night Is Coming"

All except Sundays: Go outside,
Be quiet, Don't play any games.

Other days, Come straight home.
Change your school clothes.

Go straight to the field.
There's little daylight left.

At seven, you got a hoe,
were set to weeding,

or sent to fetch
a sharpening tool.

Beware of snakes,
and the bull.

Later, behind the planting plow
you learned to hold a book.

Only thing, the hopper gave out
nine rows before you noticed.

If the mule stopped,
he received the board of education.

"Now that I have your attention,"
your pa enjoyed muttering.

Sundays he preached new heaven,
weekdays, tilled Eden's edge

with his boys encouraged
by the buggy whip

to dance toward the Kingdom
if they slacked, lallygagged.

"My Faith Looks Up to Thee"

On a telephone wire
above my head
a mockingbird swings

From his gray throat
a pouch appears
delicate, wind-riffled

Now clowns, lovers, muses
catcalls, secrets, dittos
silliness dancing with sacred

Where is she?
He glances backward,
chanting from on High.

"Sheep May Safely Graze"
with thanks to J.S. Bach for Cantata No. 208

When Nancy and I two-fluted ourselves
through the offertory,
the worshippers hadn't the faintest idea
why sheep were grazing just to the right
of the altar, their wool fuzzing around
our music stands, their little black eyes
like dotted quarter notes
guiding us onward across our page.

Eventually all safely grazed.
They did not eat lupine or death camas
from the altar bouquet, nor get blue tongue
from licking the chalice, or be struck dead
from nibbling the Host. No wolf
jumped from behind the communion table.

Toward the end, the little buggers floated out
over the congregation baa-ing and bleating,
white, black, and gray—the bellwether
clipping down the center aisle like a bride,
others jumping pews or trolling the Stations,
all observing the wakefulness of the folk.

For the folk it was serious multi-tasking,
guiltily passing on the offering plate,
or proudly contributing, all the while
wool-gathering, crossing legs, uncrossing arms,
wondering why it had suddenly come to them
to be glad that God made Bach.

"When Morning Gilds the Skies"

The day begins
with leaking birdsong,
random chirps,
pecks of notes
tasting a morning sky.
The sun, that sly one,
would have us think
he is coming to us
fast as a flaming marble
out of banks of clouds.
We know better.

It is we who must rise
to the occasion of day.
Our ascent will be steep,
roller-coasting at dawn
like teens laughing,
fresh for the ride.
At noon we'll know mere
seconds of poised gravity,
then plunge, white-knuckled,
screaming the tinnitus of soul
into the safety of sunset.

Jan Seale

Thirteen Ways of Hearing a Pipe Organ

1.
Let the music fill you with quicksilver.

2.
The sound is a cocoon.
You are the butterfly waiting inside.

3.
God has found voice on earth.

4.
At each new strain, a small shock of pleasure.

5.
Psalm 33:3 "Play skillfully with a loud noise."

6.
A thousand mosquitoes singing in chorus.

7.
Sorrow drowned in a tidal wave of notes.

8.
The laughter of fingers, the tears of feet.

9.
Pipes are ventriloquists.

10.
A giant stomping out of the house of melody.

11.
The sound of white silk.

12.
Locomotive of the instruments.

13.
May heaven's gates open with such a sound.

Jan Seale

Playing the Flute for the TMR Class

*Children admitted to the Trainable Mentally
Retarded program must have some minimal
communication ability in the form of either
speech or gestures.*
                    —education guidelines

They stumbled down their barracks steps
and bombed my car with sighs and shouts,
ancient children set for a lark.
I went smoothed and fingered, lingered on
and lifted up, up to their porch
patterned with sun on chicken wire
into their ripe dark classroom where
"doll" and "book" swam trainably abandoned
on the board until their teacher
came in flowered smock and quickly taught
the meaning of a semi-circle,
her Christmas eyes bidding me unafraid.

Sweating hands pressed every key,
worked all the levers, stroked
each millimeter of silver then let me
put it to my mouth and gave my fingers
grudging space upon the keys. So
came the holy Yankee Doodle spirit
marching and clapping and singing,
rolling on to bird calls, both hoot owls
and Pastoral Symphony warblers,

44

fire truck sirens convulsive
and night trains whistling.

Batman! Batman! they were crying
and with the half-steps of his tune one climbed
on a chair and soared off, we following like
a thousand evening bats at cave entrance,
rising, so we did it. Jingle Bells Michael
Row Your Boat Ashore Oh Susannah Don't
Mission Impossible Jesus Loves Me Home
On the Range The Real Thing
Two Little Ducks: it was time.

I dried my silver pipe and broke it
magically to pieces, laying it to sleep
in the Cinderella velvet of the box,
while they said it was pretty and they loved me
and why did I have to go. But I did,
assisted by unmeditated caresses,
driving away too much alone, leaving
the only holy pied spirit jumping,
singing, and kissing the wind.

IV. Volitions

Whether you call on God or not,
God will be with you.

—carved on Carl Jung's door in Küsnacht

The Grace of Doubt

An e-mail says the sender
will know I am ashamed of Jesus
if I do not send this praise letter
back to her and nine others.
Another writes,
"Don't waste a miracle."

I want to ask,
What if faith is other
than a promise of "Forward,"
other than a limbo of awe?

If faith is a journey,
I sometimes sit down
on a rock to rest.

I sometimes tilt my head
like a questioning pet,
eyes wide, listening up
for God's silent thunder.

Jan Seale

Graphing the National Mood

In the grid of the graph,
The space above begs, pleads us to look,
study the sky of the picture, see available space
above the narrow temples, those black statistical peaks
of the surveyed neglect, the counted crimes,
drunk drivers, persistent cancer, homeless children,
those killed in all wars in a given century,
those killed in the first eleven years of a new century.

That fifty-percent, even-steven skyline
flails a hand like an answering child,
grins the comedy of a face viewed upside down
or the lover's fleshy visage in missionary position,
makes a more interesting sunset behind mountains,
calls out the infinite ribbon of friendships, rising bread,
birds arranged on a wire, the truth of daylight
regardless of the news or the numbers.

It's the percentage of women not assaulted,
the men not perpetrating, the evenings completed,
days in the laboratory content to step backward, forward,
the greening of shoots in the burnout zone,
the child's hand patting the elder's shoulder,
colors all deriving from the earth, our eyes
rehearsing them to send to the heart's open door.

For now, what else can we do but be faithful
to the negative of peace that fills the blank?—
knowing it sprouts audacious through the clouds,
is not a void but an entity, a raft of possibility,
straining upward out of the sad majority,
containing the higher news of the day,
yearning to go off the charts.

Boomerang

Homeward bound from Australia,
my son calls from Sydney,
his voice as clear as next door.
I look to see if he might
be sitting out front in his pickup.

What day is it for you? I ask.
It's Tuesday, he says.
It's Monday here, I tell him.
He is flying on the world's biggest plane.
I will bring Tuesday to you, Mom.

He calls again, with a new schedule
for landing, and ends,
I love you like I did 45 minutes ago.

I hang up, thinking of love sent
across the earth in seconds,
how easy, some days,
to believe in God.

Jan Seale

Saying Goodnight from the Lower Bunk
to the Stars on My Grandson's Ceiling

For too many days now
I have thought of age
as a series of flounderings,
while the prime recedes inch by inch.
For too many nights now
I have lain sidewise, casing
a ceiling full of plastic solar system,
reviewing the mortality of all I love,
especially the child above me.

I have not given over to time itself
my trust. I have not felt enough
the happiness of wisdom
springing, blooming, singing,
shining out in me; I have not heard
the town bells toll the message
that my time's sweetness
is fulfilled amid my life's cacophony.

But now I turn to what is left,
beg a lingering summer's evening,
reach up to feel the gentle undersided
rhythm of my sleep-breathing grandchild,
and pray that winter's final dark
brings yards and yards of stars.

My father said,

       when he came to sit beside me,
teen me lying face down on my bed
soggy with tears about God and doubt,
"There will always be *feelings*
and always be *beliefs*. You
can't choose feelings:
they choose you.
You can choose beliefs."

He rose and diddled his fingers
gently on my back. "When
you're through with your tears,
leave them here on your bed.
Bring your beliefs to supper."

Jan Seale

The Yo-Yo Artist Lines it Out for Us

In the beginning
Gravity Pull
then
Rock the Baby
followed by
Around the World.
Afternoons,
settle for
Walk the Dog
and
Skin the Cat.
Evenings
it's
Throw-down,
then
Sleeper.

Easter Sunday

The people arose from tombs in early morning
to testify against the laws of death—
flapped grave clothes, rolled stones, shouted alleluias.
Giving diuretics to the lilies to make sure
they would excrete living scents in the sanctuary,
they clasped many a relic of a Jesus' cross,

stained walnut, plastic, lugged, swinging cross
to remind themselves that Easter was on the morning.
The janitor appeared early in the sanctuary
to disclose the doors, shoo out the night's death
of doubt, an order from the priest to make sure
there was fresh spirit blowing for alleluias.

Choirs and organs scintillating with alleluias—
the people needing song to bear their cross,
the essences to become sure
they could prove eternity this particular morning
when nothing must use the rusty patina of death.
In the resurrection they planned a sanctuary.

The stained glass panes high in the sanctuary
streamed prismatic mauve and azure alleluias.
The ad men sang, "It's a holiday for death,"
and no one lifted the slightest finger to cross
them. It was a true holiday morning
and sales that week had been good, for sure.

Christ! He knew nothing at all for sure
except his death needed no proving sanctuary
where people gathered earlier than usual Sunday morning
to listen to themselves in baroque alleluias,

to pray—eyes squeezed tight—sing, uphold the cross,
recall the illogic which denied his death.

He did not care to hear he died no death,
worshipped because what he did was a sure
thing. He wanted not for them to hunt him in the cross,
not to prove wild leaps of faith or find a sanctuary
for themselves, wild men blubbering alleluias
since the year was at its morning.

An Easter morning should be a time of death
to proving alleluias. What is sure
is no rational sanctuary in the cross.

Begging at St. Mark's

Mute light of sacerdotage
after the Adriatic glitter,
carnate pigeons, glassblower's sweat.
Gabrieli's ghost suspended in the dimness,
his dialogs of trumpets and singers
above the altar, great dome
echoing the birth pangs of antiphony.
Below, the Second Apostle,
or some donkey as surrogate, resting
inside the jeweled sarcophagus,
the glory of which could feed
a whole starving country.

We've been in line half the day,
the four bronze horses corralled
in scaffolding above us, my mate and I.
He has borne his fever like the pilgrim
he is until he's seen the birthplace
of antiphonal song. Now he sinks
at the foot of a marble pillar.
We're two hours short of our ride
and it's cooler here,
in an airless sort of way,
than outside on the treeless piazza.

I go in search of water but there's none
in this place of baptisteries and communions,
in this shrine threatened with drowning
in the sea. Dry fonts, glass whales
underfoot, schools of mosaics swimming by,
behemoths bellowing out of the Psalms—
I'm lost in antiquity. He's dry.

Circling to check him again and again,
check his passport, his pulse,
straighten him against the column,
I warn him not to sprawl. He is
too mine this afternoon, and God's,
and perhaps, if I don't watch
more than they, the international
pickpockets' circling.

Finally, I see the water: retired,
name tags in place, Methodists from Baltimore.
(Are you still there, little wren of a couple,
saying Certainly, proffering an extra cup?)
Be bold in Christ, Saint Mark calls.
So I touch her sleeve, show them my husband
reclined in a Titian slouch, red-faced as marble.

Transubstantiation in a Dixie cup,
Muslims, Buddhists, Hindus and Jews passing by.
Take, Drink, I tell my delirious man.
This is what we get for having faith.

What the Bristlecones Said
for Bob

You take me to see them, bristlecones
you discovered a summer ago.
They hang comic and grand on the edge
of a mile straight down,
Pinus Aristata, endangered species,
a stand or two in six western states.
That's all. At first I wonder what
would be lost, they are so ugly:
gray gnarled trunks suffering from sciatica,
old dogs trying to scratch themselves,
scraggly unsure heads that would have dandruff
if human, and should duck before the blue spruce.
Still, age and oddness due respect,
we count the rings of one, a section
of trunk sawed down (Only Dead Wood Is Taken,
says the sign for handmade ashtrays)
and estimate it is young—1500 years
give or take a century or two. The odd part—
the trunk is dead: the branches live.
Refusing to come down off their mountaintops,
these stubborn trees make bargain:
they'll look dead, play dead, be sort of dead
in exchange for "home," all the while smiling
in death and birthing little porcupines
glad to snag on anything for a ride
as long as it's traveling higher.
Unbelieving, we touch the branches—

splay of needles with spermy resin
not to leave our hands for hours,
stony arms impervious to rot, cool as mummies.
A mountain bluebird perches atop
one unsalable pine, July Christmas angel.
In the car, rain dredging the high country,
we eat lunch and puzzle semi-immortality.
We want life dead or alive.
Descending, reviewing the grove
sitting smug as Buddha, we ask our god
why he is playing favorites.

Futures

And yonder all before us lie
Deserts of vast eternity.

—Andrew Marvell
(1621-1678)

Dealing in Futures

The sonogram snows, then straightens
to a quarter-pie of glacial bed,
conglomerate tumbling, glowing debris.
Now a shape too sharp for chance appears,
a form swimming through glitter.
Puffy eyes, blunt nose, no chin.
It gives a charming marmot smile.

The doctor calibrates in flowers,
stop-actioning with tiny asterisks
to measure side to side, front to back.
The femur shines like a sunken ingot,
receives the blessed centimeters;
the brain lobes are twins, thank God,
and sit distinct in reason, art.

We're cool, dispassionate until we see
this spirit-life experiments with agendas:
an astronaut afloat in cabin fever,
harpist practicing arpeggios,
cyclist pedaling watery meters
on a bike not yet imagined.

While we strive to find (eyes watering
from stares or seeing our future fleshed)
a boy? a girl?—oblivious to voyeurism,
it bends to play with feet, check toes.
And then insistently declining our offer
to know its sex, it settles to taste a thumb,
and for this one last time a mystery,
to moon us.

63

Jan Seale

How to Save Time

Gather seconds from the Einstein landscape,
first cargo hangars, now medieval control tower,
then tree lines, golf course, plowed field, freeway
all aching to catch runaway planes.
Build a confession booth for the vanities
in the cargo hole: nail polish, extra shoes, fat journal.
Soon a prayer will appear, echo box of several seconds,
"I believe! I believe! Let this plane impossibly rise."

Come the day you add the roaring chord of the organ
held longer at the end of a hymn, when the organist
shows you who's boss, rubs your nose in adoration
or duty, leaves you reeling with decibels. Gather also
the silence after the final note of the symphony, when
the conductor prays against the first Bravo!
Be patient. You will find these economies useful.

Now dump in the wait at left-turn-only arrows,
before the lead car, acting on a behemoth's tip,
decides it's a go. Take your time. Home,
and peeling potatoes, stir in the interval when
the cut is foreseen and the bright blood appears.

Bedtime, include the greed of lovemaking's brief finale,
mark the beats between lightning and thunder,
then contribute the nth before sleep,
when you tell yourself you are telling yourself
you are walking through the valley of the shadow.

Someday, at your downsizing, a helper calls
from the next room, "What's to do with this box of time?"
Still your hands: Go to the call. Attend your stored moments:
They crawl out in a row like cutter ants, bear off left
for the garden humming, blinking, ticktocking.

Pre-need

There is so much work to death:
Will it be a cardboard box or reinforced steel?
Poplar, pecan, or oak . . .

although these latter cannot be sealed
since they are quite alive, still trees?
Thus, the issue is gasketed or ungasketed?

Gasketed is sealed, of course,
(like a jar of Grandmother's figs), and
"does not easily admit gravesite elements."

Heavens, no!—I don't want pink for the liner.
It must be ecru, or parchment or linen—
a color of paper, my favorite life surface.

Crepe is okay, or satin.
Last choice would be velvet
because I'm prone to hot flashes.

As for the inner lid, No thank you
on the populars: Going Home,
Virgin of Guadalupe, or Christ of the Andes.

Likewise the camouflaged liner
with the deer angel on the lid, special ordered
by a hunter who switched to cremation.

Now on to the final resting place—
Will it be "Gethsemane" or "Angel Field,"
"Mount of Olives" or "Garden of Peace"?

Take into consideration, in our area
there could be "drainage issues."
Thus, an inurnment? a mausoleum drawer?

And if it's ground burial, will it be side by side,
or stacked, and if so, how to decide,
like on warmer nights, who's on top?

Finally, the monument: marble, granite?
And of course if you will have been a Mason
or DAR, these symbols can be added.

No doubt, the way our sons grew up
questioning everything,
there will be some scoffing,

an abhorrence of the rituals,
especially the sentimental.
Still, take away the trappings,

including line items: guest book,
thank you notes, escort limo,
flower car, and these words:

"at the time of need,"
"whenever the service takes place",
"issues," and particularly "situations,"

and how else are we to get died?

Certainty

Before this second life, he knew everything,
especially what heaven was like,
and earned his living telling folks what pleasure
dying was, his time with daughters measured
out in yardsticks of piety, responsibility, and care.
The earthly coulds were under wraps of shoulds.

Sex didn't exist, except embarrassment of his:
two daughters there as the nose on his face.
At this remove, I know his supper table commands
for what they were: fear. That day some
grieving mother had poured out to him the news
of her unmarried pregnant daughter.

First, observation:
"These blackbirds here at my feeder
come several times a day to peck peck peck."
Then, apology:
"Sorry you see me like this.
I know enough to know I don't know anything."
And finally, declaration:
"I love you so very very"
and his eyes rinse out his heart.

He gave me watches for birthdays—
"Take care—especially in the rain;
Don't overwind; no dropping, no whacking. "
They lie in my jewelry box, time scrambled.

Now, if there's time, he tells me
he doesn't have the foggiest idea
what heaven is like. He says he's ready,

Jan Seale

really ready. The nights are every one too long.
Good thing he doesn't have a gun.

Days, his watch is his best friend:
"They're bringing my pills."
"It's time for the food."
"They come for the clothes in 25 minutes."

With wool socks I brought last time,
he's built a threshold under his door.
Over these we step each time we enter.
"This time of year it's crickets, crickets
 the world over, crickets by the buckets."
He smiles, the half-rhyme pleasing
some old elegant poetry-quoting place.

He consults his watch.
"One thing's for sure, honey:
you better go before they lock the door."

Jan Seale

really ready. The nights are every one too long.
Good thing he doesn't have a gun.

Days, his watch is his best friend:
"They're bringing my pills."
"It's time for the food."
"They come for the clothes in 25 minutes."

With wool socks I brought last time,
he's built a threshold under his door.
Over these we step each time we enter.
"This time of year it's crickets, crickets
 the world over, crickets by the buckets."
He smiles, the half-rhyme pleasing
some old elegant poetry-quoting place.

He consults his watch.
"One thing's for sure, honey:
you better go before they lock the door."

Jan Seale

really ready. The nights are every one too long.
Good thing he doesn't have a gun.

Days, his watch is his best friend:
"They're bringing my pills."
"It's time for the food."
"They come for the clothes in 25 minutes."

With wool socks I brought last time,
he's built a threshold under his door.
Over these we step each time we enter.
"This time of year it's crickets, crickets
 the world over, crickets by the buckets."
He smiles, the half-rhyme pleasing
some old elegant poetry-quoting place.

He consults his watch.
"One thing's for sure, honey:
you better go before they lock the door."

68

To a friend who died somewhat unexpectedly

We marked each day you coughed a little less
and noted that your color was quite good.
You did not talk of personal distress

at midnight, or the episodes of blood
upon so many things. Nor did you show
the sentimental eye which finally would

not focus or the headache much too slow
in going away. Today at last I went
to your grave. Twice I had to go back

to the gardener to ask which one he meant.
Sun bleached red of plastic roses bloomed
your second cousin had so kindly sent

two weeks before. Now, with you entombed,
I was eager to kneel and bring the tears at last,
to make a present of my grief exhumed.

But in honor of all trivia in the past,
I mindless stood, wiping sweat from my face,
and, *simpático*, agreed with you that grass
would have a problem growing in that place.

Suddenly,

    everyone is dying, going to Someplace.
I don't understand. Newly, I don't understand.
We're giving death reports to our children
the way we complained of our parents doing.
Age is knocking us up, a definite
tell-tale shade on the litmus,
formerly a speck not worth a squint.

Death's moved into the neighborhood,
made itself a welcome plate of brownies,
subscribed to the paper, built a pen for its dogs.
Lately, it's been going up and down the street
delivering letters on ways we can organize.
We're all addressed as "Resident."

Mister Samuel Overton

He did it in the space between our Sundays.
To him, it happened after only one.
Ingenious with the wrong equipment,
he built a self-extinction kit, and used it.

The local paper made an observation
on Monday evening under "Deaths"
that Mister Overton had last been seen
alive at church the night before
found dead the morning after.
We of the church mistook it for an editorial.

Some thrilled that they had spoken to,
brushed against, sat behind, beside or
directly across from—a desperate man.
Hindsight, they prophesied,
I had a feeling about him.

Others opined he had not tried to talk it over
with someone that night. So uncalled for.

One said, Well, he was old (What? Only 56?)
One said he'd been told he was sick.

Another said he had no family
so must be happy finally.

I myself felt suited to the argument
it was inevitable . . . ne'er-do-well he was.

I said Tragic, Really Tragic
and felt unsettled for almost an hour.
A day or two passed. We stored

71

Jan Seale

our Monday paper in the trash
and our Overton inside the grass.
We did it right: official organist,
his favorite hymn, respectable number
of floral off'rings, and proper amount
of congregation having struggled into
funeral clothes a weekday afternoon.

With his body gone, I can admit
I was afraid of him. When I saw him
by the hat rack in the hall,
his Bible big and shattering
like an overheated rose
it was so used, I wondered if he might
block my way, demand to know
if I was pre- or post-millennial
a question always burning just below
his mottled surface.

He wore gray suits soured lavender.
He didn't smell exactly right to others.
He didn't hear too well for himself.

He almost made me stop that final Sunday
when I sang toward him a howareyou
and pledged privately his answer would not
bother the rhythm of my steps.
He flapped his Bible arm at me as a fisherman
casts for a fish he can already see,
desperate and straining. Well . . . well, he stammered
stepping forward, Let's . . . just say . . . I'm here.

But I had books to exchange
and chairs to arrange,

and besides,
he was slightly deranged.

The widening of the hallway came that night.
Now we can pass with greater ease.

I tell myself a hat rack's not a cross;
to keep one's brother is impractical;
the old codger would, sure he would,
have refused a hundred cups of water
I might have offered.
I wisely list his problems unresolved
and lament one chronically unhappy man.

No, I could not have stopped him. But
given another time, a Mister Overton,
a hat rack and a hall somewhere,
I hope to break the rhythm of my steps
upon the stairs.

Jan Seale

In the Heaven of Nightgowns,

                     they singularly
shall not be sweated or dripped upon;
nor careless washed or other tragedy—
a sharp protrusion or door overslammed
banish them to the dread hell of the rag box.
They shall always fit themselves, never outgrown,
and have choice of positions, upright or prone.

Extra credit will be awarded for hearing prayers,
for being misused for housework or lounging,
for keeping every secret backstairs,
for acrobatics in donning; g-forces ungowning,
not speaking a word of affairs,
for keeping the proud and the sleepy hidebound,
for agreeing to being unwound and unwound

from the sleeping woman who tosses and turns.
Unsung as egg whites on earth, for now
they must content themselves with sojourns
as close to a body as she will allow,
comforting her when she yearns
half her life away, and when the bough
breaks and the cradle falls, catching her somehow.

But in the heaven of nightgowns, these lowly habits
will be the haute couture of dreams.
Forever, they'll wear their names, cohabit
as "Diaphany," "Gossamer," or "Sateen,"
or for the cold "Linsey-woolsey" or "Flannelette."
These names shall spell for them good omen:
Each sleeps, at last, eternally, her only woman.

To a late local environmentalist

You went away to die, like an ailing pet
we search the neighborhood for.
I had a new book for you,
one about our river lands,
the precious ribbon of life
you took so personally,
worked at as an antidote
for the slow poison taking you.
The book was inscribed,
"To ___, friend of all Valley creatures,
with my love and admiration."

Today I take it from its mailer,
cut out its inscription page,
tape on a note: Damaged.
Back on the shelf.
I hate the envelope,
its accusing "Return to Sender" finger,
start to toss it, but
you wouldn't want me wasting a tree.
Remember how we held that funeral
for a cluster of palms uprooted,
replaced by a discount shoe store?

Just now at dawn the red-crowned parrots
make their daily flight over my house,
their sudden hilarious screeching
saying it's *el primer día* of their world,

saying you rest in *el primer día*
of your new habitat, that you smile,
seeing the bobcat hides in his
necessary brush along the Rio Grande.

Jan Seale

Night Flight to the Valley

Preparing to land, jets now slowed, revved, slowed,
from seventy miles inland we look east to the gush
of connecting towns, carpet of gold, blue, silver lights
spilling toward the Gulf. Yes, of course, down there
are houses of cardboard, too much water or none,
tied dogs, wired children, stash houses. Still,
from six miles up, the little cities breathe fireflies,
mime the Seven Cities of Cibola, dazzle all together
like a landed galaxy. Earlier this pristine night,
the pilot has entertained: "At present, Austin is below,
soon San Antonio. Off to your left see Houston's lights."
Houston? Tonight, we are reading the map God-vantaged.

Now sharply banking to avoid the dark ribboned Rio,
the cloudy glow of a half-million war-weary Reynosans,
we fold laptops, click lights, find shoes, lick lips.
Once, I knew people on this flight, friends returning
from Dallas or San Fran. Tonight, no familiar faces. Rather,
a Chinese delegation, shopping or ailing Mexicans,
relatives of Winter Texans, a native son back from Iraq.

The attendant launches her spiel, thanking us, and
"if you have a connecting flight—(pause) oh, never mind—
(pause) this *is* your final destination (pause), or better be."
Laughter blunts the roar of landing, and, gathering up
our messy selves, we tunnel through to leave this grounding,
pray our Final Destination might be thus previewed
by a glittering stardust trail to the sea, a soft let-down,
laughter, and exit into a night of fragrant waiting flowers.

Nape

Here's praise to the nape of the neck,
a much neglected organ. Become a nape watcher

and you see strawberries stamped
at the turnstile of birth; an overhang of hair—

natural queue, leftover of the widow's peak,
or tail of a valentine, which leads me to say

the nape of the neck is a touch key of love:
feather-stroked, the whole board lights up.

The hair at the nape stays young forever.
Ancients go to their graves black-naped

which leads me to say: when I die,
I'd rather not be redeemed like a gymnast recovering

on a trampoline, springing from grave
to feet blinded by an eastern sun. Rather

let God come like a thick dumb mother cat,
pick up what's left by the nape of its neck,

and move it to safe quarters.

Jan Epton Seale, the 2012 Texas Poet Laureate, lives in the Rio Grande Valley of Texas where she writes poetry, essays, and short fiction. Seale is the author of six books of poetry, two short story collections, three books of nonfiction, and several children's books. She is the recipient of a National Endowment for the Arts fellowship in poetry and seven PEN Syndicated Fiction awards. She is a member of the Texas Institute of Letters.

www.janseale.com